Superfood Co
Delicious Clean Eating
for Easy Weight Loss and Detox

by **Alissa Noel Grey**
Text copyright(c)2017 Alissa Noel Grey

Table Of Contents

Slimming Superfood Salads To Boost Your Health

Fresh superfood salads are simply a miracle for weight loss. They are quick to make, light and flavorful, but also nourishing and energizing when prepared in the right way. Homemade superfood salads can really give you the figure of your dream and are a great meal, either as a healthy lunch, weeknight dinner or even for the festive season get-togethers. Superfood salads are the easiest filling food that can assist in your weight-loss efforts.

In my family we simply love salads and eat one every day. Prepared at home with simple vegetables, lean meats, and legumes, superfood salads are incredibly satisfying, crush carvings and will keep you energized for hours.

The easy superfood salads I am offering you in my new cookbook have been handed down from generation to generation over the years and I have personally tasted them all. Each recipe is packed with nourishing and nutrient-rich vegetables, superfood herbs and spices, whole grains, lean meats or legumes. They have been slightly adapted to suit our modern tastes and are always absolutely delicious, healthy and budget friendly.

Chicken and Broccoli Salad

Serves: 4

Prep time: 10 min

Ingredients:

2 cooked chicken breasts, diced

1 small head broccoli, cut into florets

1 cup cherry tomatoes, halved

2 tbsp olive oil

2 tbsp basil pesto

Directions:

Heat two tablespoons of olive oil in a non-stick frying pan and gently sauté broccoli for 5-6 minutes until tender.

Place broccoli in a large salad bowl. Stir in the chicken and tomatoes. Add the basil pesto, toss to combine and serve.

Vitamin Chicken Salad

Serves: 4

Prep time: 5 min

Ingredients:

3 cooked chicken breasts, shredded

2 yellow bell peppers, thinly sliced

1/2 red onion, thinly sliced

1 large green apple, peeled and thinly sliced

2 tbsp light mustard

Directions:

In a deep salad bowl, combine the onion, peppers, apple and chicken.

Stir in the mustard, refrigerate for 10 minutes, and serve.

Mashed Avocado and Chicken Salad

Serves: 4-5

Prep time: 5 min

Ingredients:

2 cooked chicken breasts, diced

1 small red onion, finely chopped

2 ripe avocados, mashed with a fork

2 tbsp olive paste

Directions:

Place the chicken in a medium sized salad bowl.

In a plate, mash the avocados using either a fork or a potato masher and add them to the chicken. Add in the onion and olive paste. Stir to combine and serve.

Mediterranean Chicken and Pasta Salad

Serves: 5-6

Prep time: 5 min

Ingredients:

3 cups small whole wheat pasta, cooked

3 chicken breast halves, cooked and shredded

1 cup cherry tomatoes, halved

1 yellow bell pepper, sliced

1 small red onion, sliced

1/2 cup black olives, pitted

2 tbsp capers

1/3 cup pine nuts, toasted

7-8 fresh basil leaves, finely chopped

for the dressing:

1/4 cup lemon juice

1/4 cup extra virgin olive oil

2 garlic cloves, crushed

salt, to taste

Directions:

Place pasta, chicken, tomatoes, bell pepper, red onion, basil, olives, capers and pine nuts in a large bowl.

Prepare the dressing by whisking lemon juice, olive oil, garlic and salt. Pour the dressing over the salad, toss to combine, and serve.

Chicken and Potato Salad with Olives

Serves: 4-5

Prep time: 5 min

Ingredients:

1 lb chicken breast halves, cooked and sliced

1 lb boiled potatoes, peeled and diced

1/2 red onion, chopped

1/4 cup black olives, pitted

1 tbsp capers

1/2 tsp ground ginger

1 tsp cumin

1 tsp paprika

1/4 tsp dried oregano

1/2 tsp salt

1/4 tsp black pepper

3 tbsp lemon juice

4 tbsp extra virgin olive oil

1/4 cup parsley leaves, chopped

Directions:

In a small glass bowl, whisk together the lemon juice, cumin, paprika, salt, black pepper, ginger, and oregano. Whisk in 4 tablespoons of the olive oil.

In a salad bowl, combine the warm potatoes with half of the dressing. Add in the sliced chicken, onion, olives, capers, parsley, and the remaining dressing, and toss to combine.

Simple Greek Chicken Salad

Serves: 4-5

Prep time: 5 min

Ingredients:

3 chicken breast halves, cooked and sliced

1 small cucumber, sliced

2 medium tomatoes, sliced

1/2 red onion, sliced

1/4 cup black olives, pitted

1 cup crumbled feta cheese

1 tsp dried oregano

1 tbsp lemon juice

2 tbsp extra virgin olive oil

1/4 cup parsley leaves, finely cut

salt, to taste

Directions:

Place the chicken, tomatoes, cucumber, red onion, olives, feta, and parsley in a salad bowl.

Toss to combine, drizzle with lemon juice and olive oil, sprinkle with oregano, toss again, and serve.

Superfood Macaroni and Beet Salad

Serves 4

Prep time 25 min

Ingredients:

2 cups macaroni

4 oz smoked salmon

1 cup roasted walnuts

2 boiled beets, peeled and diced

1 cup mayonnaise

Directions:

Cook macaroni as directed on package. When cooked through but al dente, remove from heat, drain and rinse.

Combine the macaroni, mayonnaise, salmon, walnuts and beets. Refrigerate for 10 minutes and serve.

Pea and Orzo Salad

Serves 4

Prep time 25 min

Ingredients:

1 cup orzo

2 cups frozen peas

1 cup finely cut parsley leaves

1-2 spring onions, finely cut

4 tbsp basil pesto

Directions:

Cook orzo in a large saucepan of boiling, salted water, following packet directions until tender. Add peas in the last 3 minutes of cooking. Drain well and return to pot.

Add pesto to the orzo mixture. Stir in parsley and serve.

Green Power Salad

Serves: 3-4

Prep time: 5 min

Ingredients:

2 cups mixed green salad leaves

1 cup broccoli or sunflower sprouts

1 small cucumber, chopped

1 avocado, peeled and cubed

5-6 radishes, sliced

1 tbsp chia seeds

1 tbsp pumpkin seeds

for the dressing:

1 tbsp lemon juice

1 tbsp red wine vinegar

2 tbsp extra virgin olive oil

1 tbsp Dijon mustard

salt and pepper, to taste

Directions:

Place all ingredients in a large salad bowl and toss until combined.

In a medium bowl, whisk ingredients for the dressing until smooth. Pour over salad, toss thoroughly and serve.

Walnut Pesto Chicken Salad

Serves: 4

Prep time: 10 min

Ingredients:

2 cups cooked chicken, diced

1 large apple, peeled and diced

1 large avocado, peeled and diced

for the walnut pesto

1/2 cup walnuts, chopped

10 fresh basil leaves

1 garlic clove

2-3 green olives

4 tbsp extra virgin olive oil

1 tbsp lemon juice

salt and black pepper, to taste

Directions:

In a food processor, blend together walnuts, olives, basil, olive oil, garlic and lemon juice until completely smooth.

Combine diced chicken, apple, and avocado. Pour over the walnut pesto, stir to combine and serve.

Chicken, Broccoli and Tofu Salad

Serves: 4

Prep time: 5-6 min

Ingredients:

2 lbs broccoli, cut into florets

4 oz firm tofu

1⁄2 cup red onion, chopped

1 cup cooked chicken breasts, diced

1 cup mozzarella cheese, grated

1/2 cup fresh parsley leaves, finely cut

2 tbsp extra virgin olive oil

2 tbsp soy sauce

2 tbsp lemon juice

Directions:

Steam broccoli for 4-5 minutes until just tender. Mix it with the chicken pieces.

Wrap tofu with fine cotton cloth and squeeze out to remove some water. Crumble it tofu and add it to the broccoli. Add in onion and finely cut parsley and combine very well.

In a smaller cup, mix the olive oil, soy sauce and lemon juice. Pour over the salad, toss to combine and serve.

Beef, Spinach and Avocado Salad

Serves 4-5

Prep time: 5 min

Ingredients:

8 oz quality roast beef, thinly sliced

1 avocado, peeled and sliced

1 red onion, sliced and separated into rings

2 tomatoes, thinly sliced

3 cups baby spinach

2 tbsp extra virgin olive oil

salt, to taste

for the dressing:

2 tbsp lemon juice

1 tbsp extra virgin olive oil

1 tbsp mustard

Directions:

Combine all dressing ingredients in a deep bowl and whisk until smooth.

Heat olive oil in a large skillet and gently sauté the onions and beef. Cook until the beef is heated through.

Toss together the beef, spinach, tomatoes and avocado in a large salad bowl. Season with salt, drizzle with the dressing, and serve.

Steak Salad with Arugula and Avocado

Serves 4

Prep time: 7-8 min

Ingredients:

1 lb boneless beef sirloin steak, 1 inch thick

1 avocado, peeled and sliced

3 cups arugula leaves

1 red onion, sliced and separated into rings

salt and black pepper, to taste

2 tbsp extra virgin olive oil

for the dressing:

2 garlic cloves, crushed

2 tbsp extra virgin olive oil

1 tbsp balsamic vinegar

1/2 tsp dried basil

salt and black pepper, to taste

Directions:

Prepare the dressing by whisking all ingredients in a bowl.

In a heavy skillet, heat olive oil. Season steak with salt and black pepper, and cook for 3-4 minutes, each side, on medium heat. Set aside on a cutting board and leave to cool. Slice against the grain.

Toss the steak with arugula, onion and avocado. Season with salt and pepper, drizzle with dressing, and serve.

Mediterranean Beef Salad

Serves 4-5

Prep time: 5 min

Ingredients:

8 oz quality roast beef, thinly sliced

1 avocado, peeled and diced

2 tomatoes, diced

1 cucumber, peeled and diced

1 yellow pepper, sliced

2 carrots, shredded

1 cup black olives, pitted and halved

2-3 fresh basil leaves, torn

2-3 fresh oregano leaves

1 tbsp balsamic vinegar

4 tbsp extra virgin olive oil

salt and black pepper, to taste

Directions:

Combine the avocado and all vegetables in a large salad bowl. Add in basil and oregano leaves.

Season with salt and pepper, drizzle with balsamic vinegar and olive oil and toss to combine. Top with beef and serve.

Ground Beef Salad with Creamy Avocado Dressing

Serves 4-5

Prep time: 5 min

Ingredients:

1 green lettuce, cut in stripes

2-3 green onions, finely cut

1 garlic clove, crushed

½ cup black olives, pitted and halved

4-5 radishes, sliced

8 oz ground beef, cooked

2 tbsp extra virgin olive oil

1/2 tsp ground cumin

1/2 tsp dried oregano

1 tsp paprika

salt and pepper, to taste

for the dressing:

1 avocado, peeled and cut

1 tbsp extra virgin olive oil

4 tbsp lemon juice

2 garlic cloves, cut

1 tbsp water

1/2 tsp salt

Directions:

Blend the dressing ingredients until smooth.

Heat olive oil in a medium saucepan and gently cook ground beef and seasonings. Place lettuce, cooked beef and all other salad ingredients in a bowl. Toss well to combine. Drizzle with dressing and serve.

Arugula Salad with Goat Cheese, Toasted Walnuts and Cherries

Serves: 4

Prep time: 15 min

Ingredients:

1 bunch arugula leaves

2/3 cup goat cheese, crumbled

3/4 cup dried cherries

1 1/2 cups boiling water

1/2 cup chopped parsley leaves

1/3 cup toasted walnuts

for the dressing:

1 tbsp orange juice

1 tbsp cider vinegar

2 tbsp extra virgin olive oil

salt and pepper, to taste

Directions:

Put the dried cherries in a small bowl and pour the boiling water over them. Let steep for 10 minutes, then drain.

In another small bowl, whisk together the orange juice, vinegar and olive oil. Season with salt and pepper to taste.

Put the arugula in a large serving bowl. Scatter the cherries, parsley and goat cheese over the top. Drizzle with the dressing, top with toasted walnuts, and serve immediately.

Pasta and Brussels Sprout Salad

Serves: 5-6

Prep time: 20-25 min

Ingredients:

2 cups cooked orzo

4 cups Brussels sprouts, halved

2 leeks, washed, trimmed and sliced

½ cup walnuts, chopped

½ cup dried cranberries

½ cup fresh parsley, chopped

2 tbsp balsamic vinegar

3 tbsp extra virgin olive oil

Directions:

Preheat the oven to 350 F. Line a baking tray and arrange Brussels sprouts and leeks on it. Drizzle with olive oil, balsamic vinegar and salt and toss to coat. Roast about 20-25 minutes.

In a salad bowl, toss together orzo, roasted vegetables, walnuts and cranberries. Season with salt and pepper to taste and serve.

Spinach and Asparagus Salad
with Sesame-Yogurt Dressing

Serves: 4-5

Prep time: 7 min

Ingredients:

1 bunch asparagus, woody ends trimmed, cut into 3 inch lengths

1 bag baby spinach

1 medium cucumber, peeled and sliced

for the dressing:

2 tbsp extra virgin olive oil

1 tbsp red wine vinegar

2 tbsp yogurt

2 garlic cloves, crushed

salt and pepper, to taste

1 tbsp toasted sesame seeds, to serve

Directions:

Cook the asparagus in a medium saucepan of boiling water for 3 minutes or until bright green and tender crisp. Wash with running cold water and drain well.

Whisk the oil, vinegar, yogurt and garlic in a small bowl until smooth. Season with salt and pepper to taste.

Combine the asparagus, spinach and cucumber in a large salad bowl. Drizzle with the dressing, toss to combine, sprinkle with sesame seeds and serve.

Pumpkin and Spinach Salad

Serves: 4-5

Prep time: 25 min

Ingredients:

3 cups pumpkin, deseeded, peeled and cut into wedges

1 bag baby spinach leaves

2 tbsp toasted pine nuts

1 tbsp dried cranberries

1 tbsp honey

1 tbsp sesame seeds

3 tbsp extra virgin olive oil

2 tbsp lemon juice

1 tbsp Dijon mustard

Directions:

Preheat oven to 350 F. Line a baking tray with baking paper. Place the pumpkin in a large bowl, drizzle with two tablespoons of olive oil and honey. Season with salt and pepper to taste. Toss until the pumpkin pieces are well coated. Arrange them in a single layer on the baking tray.

Bake, turning once, for 20 minutes or until golden. Remove from oven, sprinkle evenly with the sesame seeds and return to oven. Bake for 1-2 minutes or until the seeds are lightly toasted. Set aside for to cool.

Combine the lemon juice, remaining olive oil and mustard in a small bowl. Whisk until smooth. Season with salt and pepper.

Place the pumpkin, spinach, pine nuts and cranberries in a large salad bowl. Drizzle with the dressing, gently toss and serve.

Spinach, Beet and Feta Salad
with Lemon-Dill Dressing

Serves: 4-5

Prep time: 15 min

Ingredients:

3 medium beets, steamed, peeled and diced

1 bag baby spinach leaves

1/2 cup walnuts, toasted

4 oz feta, crumbled

4-5 spring onions, chopped

for the dressing:

1 garlic clove, crushed

2 tbsp extra virgin olive oil

2 tbsp lemon juice

1 tbsp finely chopped dill

Directions:

Wash the beets well, steam, peel and dice them. Arrange the spinach leaves in a large salad bowl. Scatter the beets, onions, walnuts and feta over the spinach.

In a smaller bowl or cup, combine the oil, lemon juice, garlic and dill. Whisk until smooth, season with salt and pepper and drizzle over the salad.

Spinach, Green Bean and Sun-Dried Tomato Salad

Serves: 4-5

Prep time: 7 min

Ingredients:

12 oz green beans, halved diagonally

1 bag baby spinach leaves

1 cup walnuts, halved and toasted

1 cup sun-dried tomatoes

2 tbsp pumpkin seeds

for the dressing:

3 tbsp extra virgin olive oil

2 tbsp red wine vinegar

2 garlic cloves, crushed

Directions:

Cook beans in a large saucepan of boiling salted water for one minute or until bright green. Rinse under cold running water, drain, pat dry and set aside.

Whisk oil, vinegar, garlic, salt and pepper in a small glass bowl until well combined.

Place spinach, walnuts, cooked beans and sun-dried tomatoes in a salad bowl and toss to combine. Drizzle with dressing and serve.

Roasted Red Pepper Hummus

Serves: 5-6

Prep time: 5 min

Ingredients:

3 large red peppers, deseeded and halved

1 15 oz can chickpeas, drained

1 tbsp tahini

3 tbsp extra virgin olive oil

½ lemon, juiced

1-2 small garlic cloves, chopped

1/2 tsp ground coriander

1/2 tsp cumin

1 tsp salt

water from the chickpea can

extra virgin olive oil, parsley, paprika for serving

Directions:

Preheat the grill to 400F and line a baking sheet with foil. Cut the peppers in half lengthways and place them, cut side down, on the lined tray.

Grill the peppers for 10-15 minutes or until the skins are a little burnt. Set aside in a bowl, covered for 10 minutes. Peel the skins.

Drain the chickpeas and keep the juice in a small cup. If possible, remove the skins from the chickpeas. Place the chickpeas in the blender and pulse.

Add the peppers, tahini, lemon juice, garlic, olive oil, cumin, coriander and salt, and blend until smooth, gradually adding the chickpea water to the mix until the mixture is completely smooth. To serve, top with olive oil, parsley, and sprinkle with paprika.

Arugula, Radicchio and Pomegranate Salad

Serves: 4

Prep time: 5 min

Ingredients:

1 bunch arugula leaves

1 small head radicchio, chopped

1 avocado, peeled and cubed

1/2 cup pomegranate seeds, from 1 medium pomegranate

1/3 cup hazelnuts

for the dressing:

1 tbsp honey

1 tbsp balsamic vinegar

2 tbsp extra virgin olive oil

1/2 tsp salt

Directions:

Place arugula, radicchio, avocado, hazelnuts and pomegranate seeds in a large salad bowl and gently toss to combine.

Whisk dressing ingredients until smooth, pour over the salad, serve and enjoy!

Summer Green Bean Salad

Serves: 4

Prep time: 10 min

Ingredients:

1 lb trimmed green beans, cut to 2-3 inch long pieces

1 small red onion, finely cut

1 cup cherry tomatoes, halved

1 avocado, peeled, pitted and cut

3-4 garlic cloves, chopped

1 tbsp chia seeds

4 tbsp extra virgin olive oil

3/4 cup freshly grated Parmesan cheese

salt and pepper, to taste

1 cup fresh dill, finely cut, to serve

Directions:

Steam or boil the green beans for about 3-4 minutes until crisp-tender. In a colander, wash with cold water to stop cooking, then pat dry and place in a salad bowl. Add red onion, garlic, cherry tomatoes, and avocado and sprinkle in the chia seeds. Season with lemon juice and balsamic vinegar.

Toss to coat, add in the olive oil and Parmesan cheese and toss again. Season to taste with salt and freshly ground black pepper. Refrigerate for an hour and serve sprinkled with fresh dill.

Three Bean Salad

Serves: 4

Prep time: 15 min

Ingredients:

½ cup canned chickpeas, drained and rinsed

½ cup canned kidney beans, drained and rinsed

1 lb trimmed green beans, cut to 2-3 inch long pieces

a bunch of radishes, sliced

5-6 green onions, chopped

½ cup cilantro leaves, finely cut

for the dressing:

2 tbsp honey

½ tsp ground dry mustard

1 tsp garlic powder

3 tbsp extra virgin olive oil

1/3 cup apple cider vinegar

1/4 tsp ground black pepper

Directions:

Steam or boil the green beans for about 3-4 minutes until crisp-tender. In a colander, wash with cold water to stop cooking, pat dry and place in a salad bowl.

Mix in the chickpeas, kidney beans, green onions, radishes and cilantro leaves.

In a smaller bowl, whisk together the apple cider vinegar, olive oil, honey, mustard, garlic powder, black pepper and salt. Pour over the salad and toss gently to coat. Cover, refrigerate for at least 1 hour, toss again and serve.

Beet and Bean Sprout Salad

Serves: 4

Prep time: 10 min

Ingredients:

5-6 beet greens, finely cut

2 tomatoes, sliced

1 cup bean sprouts, washed

1/2 cup pine nuts

for the dressing:

2 garlic cloves, crushed

4 tbsp lemon juice

4 tbsp extra virgin olive oil

1 tsp salt

Directions:

Place pine nuts in a small fry pan over medium heat and cook for 2 minutes, stirring regularly, or until golden. Remove from heat and set aside.

In a large salad bowl toss together beet greens, bean sprouts and tomatoes.

Whisk the olive oil, lemon juice, salt and garlic and pour it over the salad. Sprinkle with pine nuts, and serve chilled.

Beet Salad with Minty Yogurt Dressing

Serves: 4

Prep time: 25 min

Ingredients:

4 medium beets, steamed and cubed

1 cup strained yogurt

2 garlic cloves, crushed

1 tsp lemon juice

2 tbsp olive oil

1/2 tsp dried mint

½ tsp salt

Directions:

Wash the beets, trim the stems, and steam them over boiling water until cooked through. Plunge the beets in cold water, and peel when they are cool enough to handle. Peel and pat dry with a paper towel. Cut the beets in small cubes and place them in a deep salad bowl.

Whisk the yogurt with garlic, mint, olive oil and lemon juice in a small bowl. Pour over other ingredients and toss to combine. Serve cold.

Smoked Salmon Pasta Salad

Serves 5-6

Prep time 25 min

Ingredients:

2 cups small pasta

4 oz smoked salmon, shredded

1 orange pepper, chopped

1/2 cup finely chopped celery

1 avocado, peeled and diced

4-5 spring onions, finely cut

1/3 cup mayonnaise

2 tbsp lemon juice

salt and freshly ground black pepper, to taste

Directions:

Cook pasta as directed on package. When cooked through but al dente, remove from heat, drain and rinse.

Combine mayonnaise, lemon juice, oil and salt and pepper in a cup.

Add salmon, pepper, celery and avocado to pasta. Pour over dressing and toss until well combined.

Warm Broccoli Pasta Salad

Serves 5-6

Prep time 25 min

Ingredients:

2 cups penne

4 oz Italian sausage

2 cups broccoli florets

1 small onion, finely cut

2 garlic cloves, chopped

2 tbsp lemon juice

salt and freshly ground black pepper, to taste

Directions:

In a skillet, cook the sausages for 10-12 minutes or until cooked through and golden brown. Add in the onion and garlic and cook for 3-4 minutes.

Cook the broccoli in boiling water fo3-4 minutes until tender.

Cook pasta as directed on package. When cooked through but al dente, remove from heat, drain and rinse.

Chop the sausages into pieces and toss with the pasta, broccoli and the the cooked onions and garlic. Toss everything together well with the lemon juice and season with salt and black pepper to taste.

Warm Beet and Lentil Salad

Serves: 5-6

Prep time: 10 min

Ingredients:

1 14 oz can brown lentils, drained, rinsed

1 14 oz can sliced pickled beets, drained

1 cup baby arugula leaves

1 small red onion, chopped

2 garlic cloves, crushed

6 oz feta cheese, crumbled

1 tbsp extra virgin olive oil

for the dressing

3 tbsp extra virgin olive oil

1 tbsp red wine vinegar

1 tsp summer savory

salt and black pepper, to taste

Directions:

Heat one tablespoon of olive oil in a frying pan and gently sauté onion for 2-3 minutes or until softened. Add in garlic, lentils and beets. Cook, stirring, for 2 minutes.

Whisk together remaining olive oil, vinegar, summer savory, salt and pepper. Add to the lentils and toss to coat. Combine baby arugula, feta and lentil mixture in a bowl. Toss gently to combine and serve.

Carrot, Chickpea and Turnip Salad

Serves: 4

Prep time: 15 min

Ingredients:

7 oz carrots, shredded

5 oz white turnips, shredded

1 cup cooked chickpeas

1 tbsp sesame seeds

1 garlic clove, pressed

½ a bunch of parsley, finely cut

2 tbsp white vinegar

2 tbsp extra virgin olive oil

salt and black pepper, to taste

Directions:

Combine carrots and turnip in a large salad bowl. Add in sesame seeds, chickpeas, salt, vinegar and olive oil. Stir in parsley and garlic.

Set aside for 5 minutes, stir again and serve.

Tuna Salad with Lettuce and Chickpeas

Serves: 4

Prep time: 5 min

Ingredients:

1 head green lettuce, cut in thin strips

1 cup chopped watercress

1 cucumber, peeled and chopped

1 tomato, diced

1 can tuna, drained and broken into small chunks

1/2 cup chickpeas, from a can

7-8 radishes, sliced

3-4 spring onions, chopped

juice of half lemon

3 tbsp extra virgin olive oil

Directions:

Mix all the vegetables in a large bowl. Add the tuna and the chickpeas and season with lemon juice, olive oil, and salt to taste.

Roasted Vegetable Salad with Chickpeas

Serves: 4-5

Prep time: 30 min

Ingredients:

3 tomatoes, halved

1 zucchini, quartered

1 fennel bulb, thinly sliced

1 head broccoli, cut into florets

1 large red pepper, halved, deseeded, cut into strips

2 medium onions, quartered

1 can chickpeas, drained

1 tsp oregano

2 tbsp extra virgin olive oil

for the dressing

2/3 cup yogurt

1 tbsp fresh lemon juice

1 small garlic clove, chopped

Directions:

Place the zucchini, broccoli, pepper, fennel, onions, tomatoes and olive oil on a lined baking sheet. Season with salt, pepper and oregano and roast in a 500 degrees F oven until golden, about 20 minutes.

Whisk the yogurt, lemon juice and garlic in a bowl. Taste and season with salt and pepper. Divide the vegetables and chickpeas in 4-5 plates. Top with the yogurt mixture and serve.

Chickpea and Roasted Root Vegetable Salad

Serves: 4-5

Prep time: 30 min

Ingredients:

6 medium parsnips, peeled and halved lengthways

a bunch baby carrots, peeled and halved lengthways

4-5 medium potatoes, peeled and quartered

2 medium onions, quartered

1 can chickpeas, drained

1 tsp oregano

2 tbsp extra virgin olive oil

for the dressing

2/3 cup yogurt

1 tbsp Dijon mustard

1 small garlic clove, chopped

Directions:

Place the parsnips, carrots, potatoes and onions on a lined baking sheet. Season with salt, pepper and oregano and sprinkle with olive oil. Roast in a 500 F oven until golden, about 35 minutes.

Add in chickpeas, toss, and roast for 10 minutes more or until the chickpeas are beginning to crisp.

Whisk the yogurt, mustard and garlic in a bowl. Divide the vegetables and chickpeas in 4-5 plates. Top with the yogurt-mustard mixture and serve.

Warm Leek and Sweet Potato Salad

Serves 4-5

Prep time: 30 min

Ingredients:

1.5 lb sweet potato, unpeeled, cut into 1 inch pieces

4 small leeks, trimmed and cut into 1 inch slices

5-6 white mushrooms, halved

1 cup baby arugula leaves

2 tbsp extra virgin olive oil

for the dressing

½ cup yogurt

1 tbsp Dijon mustard

Directions:

Preheat oven to 350 F. Line a baking tray with baking paper. Place the sweet potato, leeks and mushrooms on the baking tray. Drizzle with olive oil and toss to coat. Roast for 20 minutes or until golden.

Combine yogurt and mustard in a small bowl or cup. Place vegetables, mushrooms and baby arugula in a salad bowl and toss to combine. Serve drizzled with the yogurt mixture.

Mediterranean Avocado Salad

Serves: 5-6

Prep time: 10 min

Ingredients:

2 avocados, peeled, halved and cut into cubes

½ ciabatta roll, cut into small cubes

2 cups cherry tomatoes, halved

½ red onion, thinly sliced

1 large cucumber, halved, sliced

½ cup green olives, pitted, halved

½ cup black olives, pitted, sliced

6 oz feta cheese, cut into cubes

7-8 fresh basil leaves, torn

½ cup parsley leaves, finely cut

4 tbsp extra virgin olive oil

3 tbsp red wine vinegar

Directions:

Line a baking tray with baking paper and place ciabatta cubes. Drizzle with one tablespoon of olive oil. Season with salt and pepper and gently toss to coat. Cook under the grill for 2-3 minutes or until golden. Set aside to cool.

Place all vegetables, feta, basil, olives, and ciabatta cubes in a large salad bowl. Gently toss to combine then sprinkle with vinegar and remaining olive oil. Season with salt and pepper and gently toss again. Sprinkle with parsley and serve.

Easy Artichoke and Bean Salad

Serves: 5-6

Prep time: 15 min

Ingredients:

1 14 oz can white beans, drained

2-3 large handfuls podded broad beans

3 marinated artichoke hearts, quartered

for the dressing:

2 tbsp extra virgin olive oil

1 tbsp lemon juice

1 tbsp apple cider vinegar

1 tbsp fresh mint, chopped

salt and pepper, to taste

Directions:

Cook the broad beans in boiling, unsalted water for 2-3 minutes or until tender. Drain and refresh under running cold water. Combine with the white beans and quartered marinated artichoke hearts in a large salad bowl.

In a smaller bowl, whisk olive oil, lemon juice, vinegar and mint. Pour over the bean mixture. Season with salt and pepper and toss gently to combine.

Artichoke, Mushroom and Tomato Salad

Serves: 4-5

Prep time: 15 min

Ingredients:

1 14 oz can artichoke hearts, drained, cut quartered

7-8 white mushrooms, halved

½ cup sun-dried tomatoes, halved

½ cup walnuts, halved and toasted

1 bag baby arugula leaves

2 tbsp lemon juice

1 tbsp extra virgin olive oil

salt and pepper, to taste

Directions:

Place the artichokes, mushrooms, walnuts and tomatoes in a large bowl and set aside for 5-6 minutes.

Whisk the lemon juice and olive oil in a small bowl until smooth.

Add the baby arugula leaves to the artichoke mixture. Drizzle with dressing, season with salt and pepper and toss gently before serving.

Healthy Winter Pasta Salad

Serves: 4

Prep time: 15 min

Ingredients:

2 cups cooked orzo

1-2 small beets, peeled, boiled and grated

1 apple, peeled and shredded

2 gherkins, chopped

1 small turnip, grated

3-4 spring onions, finely cut

½ bunch of fresh parsley, finely cut

2 tbsp lemon juice

3 tbsp extra virgin olive oil

salt, to taste

Directions:

Steam the beets in a basket over a pot of boiling water for about 12-15 minutes, or until tender. Leave them to cool then grate and put them in a salad bowl. Add in the finely cut spring onions, the shredded apple and turnip, the gherkins and the fresh parsley. Toss to combine.

Season with salt, lemon juice and olive oil, add in orzo, toss to combine and serve.

Easy Vitamin Salad

Serves: 4-5

Prep time: 10 min

Ingredients:

6 small new potatoes

1 carrot, peeled and cut

7 oz cauliflower, cut into florets

7 oz baby Brussels sprouts, trimmed

3-4 broccoli florets

for the dressing:

3 tbsp fresh lemon juice

2 tbsp extra virgin olive oil

2 garlic cloves, crushed

Directions:

Cook potatoes in a steamer basket over boiling water for 10 minutes or until just tender. Add in the cauliflower, broccoli and Brussels sprouts and cook for 5 minutes more. Using a vegetable peeler, cut thin ribbons from carrot. Add to the steam basket and cook for 4 minutes more. Refresh under cold running water and set aside for to cool.

Whisk the lemon juice, oil, and garlic in a small bowl. Season with salt and pepper.

Cut the potatoes in half lengthwise and place them in a salad bowl. Add in cauliflower, Brussels sprouts, carrot and broccoli. Pour the dressing over the salad and gently toss to combine.

Rainbow Superfood Salad

Serves: 4-5

Prep time: 10 min

Ingredients:

2 cups shredded red cabbage

1 cup broccoli or sunflower sprouts

1 medium cucumber

1 red apple

1 carrot, peeled

for the dressing:

1 tbsp red wine vinegar

2 tbsp extra virgin olive oil

1 tsp sumac

salt and pepper, to taste

Directions:

Using a vegetable peeler, cut thin ribbons from carrot, cucumber and apple. Place in a large bowl. Add cabbage and sprouts.

Whisk ingredients for the dressing until smooth. Pour over salad, toss to combine and serve.

Avocado, Black Bean and Red Pepper Salad

Serves: 4-5

Prep time: 6-7 min

Ingredients:

2 avocados, peeled and diced

1 can black beans, drained

2 red bell pepper, diced

1-2 green onions, finely chopped

3 tbsp lemon juice

Directions:

Place avocados, beans, bell peppers, green onions, garlic, coriander and cumin in a salad bowl. Sprinkle with lemon juice and olive oil, toss to combine and serve immediately.

Spicy Carrot Salad

Serves: 4

Prep time: 10 min

Ingredients:

4 carrots, shredded

1 apple, peeled, cored and shredded

2 garlic cloves, crushed

1/2 cup fresh dill, very finely cut

1 tbsp sesame seeds

2 tbsp lemon juice

1 tbsp honey

1/2 tsp cumin

1/2 tsp grated ginger

salt and pepper, to taste

Directions:

Combine all ingredients in a deep salad bowl.

Toss to combine, chill for 30 minutes, top with sesame seeds and serve.

Warm Tomato Salad

Serves: 4-5

Prep time: 10 min

Ingredients:

4 tomatoes, sliced

1 cup cherry tomatoes, halved

½ small red onion, very finely cut

2 garlic cloves, crushed

1 tbsp dried mint

2 tbsp extra virgin olive oil

1 tbsp balsamic vinegar

Directions:

Gently heat oil in a non-stick frying pan over low heat. Cook garlic and tomatoes, stirring occasionally, for 4-5 minutes or until tomatoes are warm but firm. Remove from heat and place in a plate.

Add in red onion, vinegar and dried mint. Season with salt and pepper to taste and serve.

Shredded Kale and Brussels Sprout Salad

Serves: 4-6

Prep time: 20 min

Ingredients:

18-29 Brussels sprouts, shredded

1 cup finely shredded kale

1/2 cup grated Parmesan or Pecorino cheese

1 cup walnuts, halved, toasted

1/2 cup dried cranberries

for the dressing:

6 tbsp extra virgin olive oil

2 tbsp apple cider vinegar

1 tbsp Dijon mustard

salt and pepper, to taste

Directions:

Shred the Brussels sprouts and kale in a food processor or mandolin. Toss them in a bowl, top with toasted walnuts, cranberries and grated cheese.

In a smaller bowl, whisk the olive oil, apple cider vinegar and mustard until smooth. Pour the dressing over the salad, stir and serve.

Tuna Pasta Salad

Serves 5-6

Prep time 25 min

Ingredients:

2 cups small pasta

2 hard boiled eggs, peeled and diced

1 can tuna in oil, drained, flaked

1 cup cherry tomatoes, halved

1 cucumber, peeled and diced

1-2 spring onions, finely cut

2 tbsp fresh parsley, chopped

3 tbsp extra virgin olive oil

2 tbsp lemon juice

1 tsp lemon zest

salt and freshly ground black pepper, to taste

Directions:

Cook pasta as directed on package. When cooked through but al dente, remove from heat, drain and rinse.

Combine lemon zest, lemon juice, oil and salt and pepper in a cup.

Add tuna, eggs, tomatoes, cucumber and parsley to pasta. Pour over dressing and toss until well combined.

Tuna and Mushroom Pasta Salad

Serves 5-6

Prep time 25 min

Ingredients:

2 cups small pasta

10 white button mushrooms, sliced

1 can tuna in oil, drained, flaked

1 red pepper, chopped

1 large apple, peeled and diced

4-5 spring onions, finely cut

1/3 cup mayonnaise

2 tbsp lemon juice

salt and freshly ground black pepper, to taste

Directions:

Cook pasta as directed on package. When cooked through but al dente, remove from heat, drain and rinse.

Combine mayonnaise, lemon juice, oil and salt and pepper in a cup.

Add tuna, apple, pepper and mushrooms to pasta. Pour over dressing and toss until well combined.

Fresh Quinoa Salad

Serves: 4-5

Prep time: 15 min

Ingredients:

1 cup quinoa, rinsed

2 cups water

1 large cucumber, diced

1 big tomato, diced

1 yellow pepper, chopped

6-7 arugula leaves

½ cup fresh dill, finely cut

for the dressing:

3 tbsp lemon juice

3 tbsp extra virgin olive oil

salt and black pepper, to taste

Directions:

Wash quinoa in a fine mesh strainer under running water for 1-2 minutes, then set aside to drain. Bring water to a boil in a medium saucepan over high heat. Add the quinoa and return to a boil. Cover, reduce heat to a simmer and cook gently for 15 minutes. Set aside, covered, for 5-6 minutes, then transfer to a large bowl.

Add the cucumber, tomato, pepper, arugula and dill. I a small bowl, combine the lemon juice, olive oil, salt and black pepper. Pour over the salad and toss to combine.

Spring Quinoa Salad

Serves: 4

Prep time: 15 min

Ingredients:

1 cup quinoa

2 cups water

5-6 green lettuce leaves, cut in stripes

a bunch of green onions, chopped

a bunch of radishes, sliced

1 cucumber, sliced in half lengthwise and cut

½ cup green olives, pitted, halved

3-4 fresh basil leaves

2 tbsp extra virgin olive oil

4 tbsp fresh lemon juice

salt, to taste

Directions:

Wash quinoa in a fine mesh strainer under running water for 1-2 minutes, then set aside to drain. Bring water to a boil in a medium saucepan over high heat. Add in the quinoa and return to a boil. Cover, reduce heat to a simmer and cook gently for 15 minutes. Set aside, covered, for 5-6 minutes, then transfer to a salad bowl.

Add in the chopped vegetables, green olives and fresh basil leaves and stir until well combined. Add salt, lemon juice and olive oil, toss and serve.

Quinoa, Black Bean and Egg Salad

Serves: 4-5

Prep time: 15 min

Ingredients:

1 cup quinoa

2 cups water

1 cup canned black beans, drained

1 tomato, sliced

2-3 green onions, chopped

2 eggs, hard boiled, peeled and sliced

½ cup fresh cilantro, finely cut

1 tsp dried mint

3 tbsp lemon juice

4 tbsp extra virgin olive oil

½ tsp salt

Directions:

Wash quinoa in a fine sieve under running water for 2-3 minutes, or until water runs clear. Set aside to drain, then boil in two cups of water for 15 minutes.

Put beans, tomato, green onions, eggs and cilantro in a bowl and toss with lemon juice, olive oil, dried mint and salt. Add in quinoa and toss to combine. Serve and Enjoy!

Cauliflower Pasta Salad

Serves 5-6

Prep time 25 min

Ingredients:

1 cup small pasta

3 cups small cauliflower florets

5 tbsp low-fat crème fraîche

3 garlic cloves, chopped

3 tbsp finely cut dill

3 tbsp extra virgin olive oil

salt and freshly ground black pepper, to taste

5 tbsp Parmesan cheese, to serve

Directions:

In a skillet, heat the olive oil and cook the cauliflower florets for 10 minutes, or until they are cooked through and tender.

Cook the pasta as directed on package. When cooked through but al dente, remove from heat, drain and rinse.

Toss with the crème fraîche, garlic, dill and cauliflower. Season with salt and pepper to taste and serve sprinkled with Parmesan cheese.

Quinoa, Kale and Roasted Pumpkin

Serves: 4-5

Prep time: 30-35 min

Ingredients:

1 cup quinoa

2 cups water

1.5 lb pumpkin, peeled and seeded, cut into cubes

2 cups fresh kale, chopped

5 oz crumbled feta cheese

1 large onion, finely chopped

4-5 tbsp extra virgin olive oil

1 tsp finely grated ginger

½ tsp cumin

Directions:

Preheat oven to 350 F. Line a baking tray and arrange the pumpkin cubes on on it. Drizzle with 2-3 tablespoons of olive oil and salt. Toss to coat, place in the oven and cook for 20-25 minutes, stirring every 10 minutes.

Heat the remaining olive oil in a large saucepan over medium-high heat. Gently sauté onion, for 2-3 minutes, or until softened. Add the spices and cook, stirring, for 1 minute more.

Wash quinoa under running water until the water runs clear. Bring two cups of water to a boil and add quinoa. Reduce heat to low, cover, and simmer for 15 minutes. Stir in kale and cook until it wilts. Gently combine quinoa and kale mixture with the roasted pumpkin and sautéed onion.

Quinoa and Brussels Sprout Salad

Serves: 5-6

Prep time: 20-25 min

Ingredients:

1 cup quinoa

2 cups water

4 cups Brussels sprouts, halved

2 leeks, washed, trimmed and sliced

½ cup walnuts, chopped

½ cup dried cranberries

½ cup fresh parsley, chopped

2 tbsp balsamic vinegar

3 tbsp extra virgin olive oil

Directions:

Preheat the oven to 350 F. Line a baking tray and arrange Brussels sprouts and leeks on it. Drizzle with olive oil, balsamic vinegar and salt and toss to coat. Roast about 20-25 minutes.

Wash quinoa under running water until the water runs clear. Bring two cups of water to a boil and add quinoa. Reduce heat to low, cover, and simmer for 10 minutes then fluff with a fork and set aside.

In a salad bowl, toss together the quinoa, roasted vegetables, walnuts and cranberries. Season with salt and pepper to taste and serve.

Buckwheat Salad with Broccoli and Roasted Peppers

Serves: 4

Prep time: 25 min

Ingredients:

1 cup buckwheat groats

1 3/4 cups vegetable broth

1 small broccoli head, cut into florets

2-3 roasted bell peppers, peeled and cut

1 red onion, finely chopped

3 garlic cloves, crushed or chopped

1 tbsp balsamic vinegar

2-3 tbsp extra virgin olive oil

½ cup fresh dill, finely cut, to serve

salt and black pepper, to taste

Directions:

Toast the buckwheat in a dry saucepan for about 2 minutes, stirring. Bring the vegetable broth to a boil and add it gently to the buckwheat. Reduce heat, cover, and simmer for 5 minutes, or until the buckwheat is tender. Remove from heat and fluff with a fork.

Arrange broccoli on a baking sheet and drizzle with garlic, olive oil, balsamic vinegar and salt. Toss to coat. Roast in a preheated to 350 F oven for about 20 minutes, or until tender. Transfer the broccoli in a large salad bowl along with the roasted peppers and buckwheat. Stir in red onion. Sprinkle with dill and toss gently.

Easy Chickpea Salad

Serves: 3-4

Prep time: 2-3 min

Ingredients:

1 15 oz can chickpeas, drained

1 medium red onion, finely cut

1 cucumber, peeled and diced

2 tomatoes, sliced

a bunch of radishes, sliced

½ cup fresh parsley, finely chopped

2 tbsp extra virgin olive oil

1 tbsp balsamic vinegar

salt, to taste

4 oz crumbled feta cheese, to serve

Directions:

In a salad bowl, toss together the chickpeas, onion, cucumber, tomatoes, radishes and parsley. Add in the balsamic vinegar, olive oil and salt and stir.

Serve sprinkled with crumbled feta cheese.

Turkey Quinoa Salad

Serves: 4

Prep time: 10 min

Ingredients:

1/2 cup quinoa

1 cup water

1 cup skinless lean turkey breast, cooked, diced

1/2 red onion, chopped

1⁄2 cup dried cranberries

1⁄2 cup walnuts

1 cup soy bean sprouts

2 tbsp extra virgin olive oil

1 tbsp lemon juice

salt and black pepper, to taste

Directions:

Wash quinoa with lots of water and boil it according to package directions.

Set aside in a salad bowl and fluff with a fork. Add in turkey, onion, cranberries and walnuts and toss to combine.

Whisk olive oil, lemon juice, salt and pepper in a separate bowl and pour over the salad. Sprinkle with soy bean sprouts, toss again, and serve.

Summer Pasta Salad

Serves 4

Prep time: 25 min

Ingredients:

2 cups small pasta

2 hard boiled eggs, peeled and diced

1 cup ham, diced

10 gherkins, diced

1/2 cup mayonnaise

Directions:

Cook pasta as directed on package. When cooked through but al dente, remove from heat, drain and rinse.

Combine the ham, pasta and all other ingredients. Stir, refrigerate for 30 minutes, and serve.

Moroccan Tomato Salad

Serves: 4-5

Prep time: 5 min

Ingredients:

2 lbs ripe tomatoes, peeled and diced

1 celery rib, diced

1 red onion, finely cut

1 green bell pepper, finely cut

2 tbsp capers

1 tsp dried mint

1 tbsp grated lemon peel

2 tbsp lemon juice

3 tbsp extra virgin olive oil

salt and black pepper, to taste

Directions:

In a deep salad bowl, toss the tomatoes with the celery, onion, green bell pepper, lemon peel and capers.

Season with dried mint, salt and black pepper to taste. Drizzle with lemon juice and olive oil and toss to combine. Refrigerate for at least 30 minutes before serving.

FREE BONUS RECIPES:
20 Superfood Paleo and Vegan Smoothies
for Vibrant Health and Easy Weight Loss

Kale and Kiwi Smoothie

Serves: 2

Prep time: 2-3 min

Ingredients:

2-3 ice cubes

1 cup orange juice

1 small pear, peeled and chopped

2 kiwi, peeled and chopped

2-3 kale leaves

2-3 dates, pitted

Directions:

Combine all ingredients in a high speed blender and blend until smooth.

Delicious Broccoli Smoothie

Serves: 2

Prep time: 2-3 min

Ingredients:

2-3 frozen broccoli florets

1 cup coconut milk

1 banana, peeled and chopped

1 cup pineapple, cut

1 peach, chopped

1 tsp cinnamon

Directions:

Combine all ingredients in a high speed blender and blend until smooth.

Papaya Smoothie

Serves: 2

Prep time: 2-3 min

Ingredients:

2-3 frozen broccoli florets

1 cup orange juice

1 small ripe avocado, peeled, cored and diced

1 cup papaya

1 cup fresh strawberries

Directions:

Combine all ingredients in a high speed blender and blend until smooth.

Beet and Papaya Smoothie

Serves: 2

Prep time: 2-3 min

Ingredients:

3-4 ice cubes

1 cup orange juice

1 banana, peeled and chopped

1 cup papaya

1 small beet, peeled and cut

Directions:

Combine all ingredients in a high speed blender and blend until smooth.

Lean Green Smoothie

Serves: 2

Prep time: 2-3 min

Ingredients:

1 frozen banana, chopped

1 cup orange juice

2-3 kale leaves, stems removed

1 small cucumber, peeled and chopped

1/2 cup fresh parsley leaves

½ tsp grated ginger

Directions:

Combine all ingredients in a high speed blender and blend until smooth.

Easy Antioxidant Smoothie

Serves: 2

Prep time: 2-3 min

Ingredients:

2-3 frozen broccoli florets

1 cup orange juice

2 plums, cut

1 cup raspberries

1 tsp ginger powder

Directions:

Combine all ingredients in a high speed blender and blend until smooth.

Healthy Purple Smoothie

Serves: 2

Prep time: 2-3 min

Ingredients:

2-3 frozen broccoli florets

1 cup water

1/2 avocado, peeled and chopped

3 plums, chopped

1 cup blueberries

Directions:

Combine all ingredients in a high speed blender and blend until smooth.

Mom's Favorite Kale Smoothie

Serves: 2

Prep time: 2-3 min

Ingredients:

2-3 ice cubes

1½ cup orange juice

1 green small apple, cut

½ cucumber, chopped

2-3 leaves kale

½ cup raspberries

Directions:

Combine all ingredients in a high speed blender and blend until smooth.

Creamy Green Smoothie

Serves: 2

Prep time: 2-3 min

Ingredients:

1 frozen banana

1 cup coconut milk

1 small pear, chopped

1 cup baby spinach

1 cup grapes

1 tbsp coconut butter

1 tsp vanilla extract

Directions:

Combine all ingredients in a high speed blender and blend until smooth.

Strawberry and Arugula Smoothie

Serves: 2

Prep time: 2-3 min

Ingredients:

2 cups frozen strawberries

1 cup unsweetened almond milk

10-12 arugula leaves

1/2 tsp ground cinnamon

Directions:

Combine ice, almond milk, strawberries, arugula and cinnamon in a high speed blender. Blend until smooth and serve.

Emma's Amazing Smoothie

Serves: 2

Prep time: 2-3 min

Ingredients:

1 frozen banana, chopped

1 cup orange juice

1 large nectarine, sliced

1/2 zucchini, peeled and chopped

2-3 dates, pitted

Directions:

Combine all ingredients in a high speed blender and blend until smooth.

Good-To-Go Morning Smoothie

Serves: 2

Prep time: 2-3 min

Ingredients:

1 cup frozen strawberries

1 cup apple juice

1 banana, chopped

1 cup raw asparagus, chopped

1 tbsp ground flaxseed

Directions:

Combine all ingredients in a high speed blender and blend until smooth.

Endless Energy Smoothie

Serves: 2

Prep time: 2-3 min

Ingredients:

1 frozen banana, chopped

11/2 cup green tea

1 cup chopped pineapple

2 raw asparagus spears, chopped

1 lime, juiced

1 tbsp chia seeds

Directions:

Combine all ingredients in a high speed blender and blend until smooth.

High-fibre Fruit Smoothie

Serves: 2

Prep time: 2-3 min

Ingredients:

1 frozen banana, chopped

1 cup orange juice

2 cups chopped papaya

1 cup shredded cabbage

1 tbsp chia seeds

Directions:

Combine all ingredients in a high speed blender and blend until smooth.

Nutritious Green Smoothie

Serves: 2

Prep time: 2-3 min

Ingredients:

2-3 frozen broccoli florets

1 cup apple juice

1 large pear, chopped

1 kiwi, peeled and chopped

1 cup spinach leaves

1-2 dates, pitted

Directions:

Combine all ingredients in a high speed blender and blend until smooth.

Apricot, Strawberry and Banana Smoothie

Serves: 2

Prep time: 2-3 min

Ingredients:

1 frozen banana

11/2 cup almond milk

5 dried apricots

1 cup fresh strawberries

Directions:

Combine all ingredients in a high speed blender and blend until smooth.

Spinach and Green Apple Smoothie

Serves: 2

Prep time: 2-3 min

Ingredients:

3-4 ice cubes

1 cup unsweetened almond milk

1 banana, peeled and chopped

2 green apples, peeled and chopped

1 cup raw spinach leaves

3-4 dates, pitted

1 tsp grated ginger

Directions:

Combine all ingredients in a high speed blender and blend until smooth.

Superfood Blueberry Smoothie

Serves: 2

Prep time: 2-3 min

Ingredients:

2-3 cubes frozen spinach

1 cup green tea

1 banana

2 cups blueberries

1 tbsp ground flaxseed

Directions:

Combine all ingredients in a high speed blender and blend until smooth.

Zucchini and Blueberry Smoothie

Serves: 2

Prep time: 2-3 min

Ingredients:

1 cup frozen blueberries

1 cup unsweetened almond milk

1 banana

1 zucchini, peeled and chopped

Directions:

Combine all ingredients in a high speed blender and blend until smooth.

Tropical Spinach Smoothie

Serves: 2

Prep time: 2-3 min

Ingredients:

1/2 cup crushed ice or 3-4 ice cubes

1 cup coconut milk

1 mango, peeled and diced

1 cup fresh spinach leaves

4-5 dates, pitted

1/2 tsp vanilla extract

Directions:

Combine all ingredients in a high speed blender and blend until smooth.

About the Author

Alissa Grey is a fitness and nutrition enthusiast who loves to teach people about losing weight and feeling better about themselves. She lives in a small French village in the foothills of a beautiful mountain range with her husband, three teenage kids, two free spirited dogs, and various other animals.

Alissa is incredibly lucky to be able to cook and eat natural foods, mostly grown nearby, something she's done since she was a teenager. She enjoys yoga, running, reading, hanging out with her family, and growing organic vegetables and herbs.

Made in United States
Orlando, FL
13 August 2023

36037375R00055